LICP

Library Instructional Computer Process

Created by Frank -N

Library (Volunteer)

Power   Energy   Success

About LICP - *Leading by Example*

Licp (***Library Instructional Computer Process***) has set designs to aid individuals by getting them the results they need quickly. Our step by step guidance and picture system takes the guess work out and shows you exactly where to point and click.

LICP is self-teaching, meaning after a short period you will find yourself recalling these step from memory. Inside this book, you will find computer help on Resume, Microsoft Word, Adobe, printing tips, email, /websites and much more.

Everyone can learn something new out of the LICP helpful guide, happy computer learning your Library Volunteer Frank -N.

Contents

Introduction:

Section 1

Section 2

Section 3

LCD: Stands for "Liquid Crystal Display." Used mostly for computers and for the newer flat screens.

CRT: Stands for "Cathode Ray Tube." Used mostly for glass screens such as the older Television set.

Hand mouse and computer Pointer

1. **Left-Click:** This is your Primary Button, used for single and Double Clicking, drag and drop with roll over object features.

2. **Right-Click:** Secondary Button, use for revealing a drop down window. When you right click on an item the drop down window will appear with a list of options.

3. **Middle Wheel:** Scroll button, for moving your computer page up or down. This feature may be "obsolete" with newer mouse devices and laptops.

4. **Mouse Pointer Arrow:** Mimics the movement of the physical mouse.

5. **Mouse Pointer Hand:** The Hand appears for a limited time only, to bring attention to: Word(s), web Link(s), picture(s), and video(s).

* The hand transform back into an arrow once it's taken off the current object.

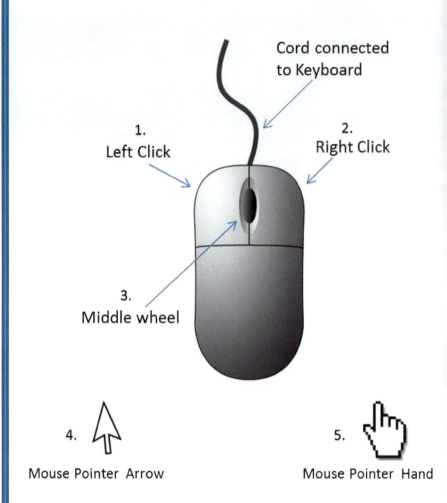

Cord connected to Keyboard

1.
Left Click

2.
Right Click

3.
Middle wheel

4. Mouse Pointer Arrow

5. Mouse Pointer Hand

Computer Keyboard: What you should know

Esc

Cap Lock

Tab

Function Keys F1-F12

Backspace

Enter Key

Number Lock

Shift

Ctrl

Window Key

Alt

Space Bar

Arrow keys

Number Pad

Time saving Tips & Writing Shortcuts

Functions-Keys for Internet

Try out these Time Saving Functions in Google or Bing

1. **F1-** Internet / windows help
2. **F3-** Opens the "find" box
3. **F5-** Refresh the web page

4. **F6-** Highlights Google search bar
5. **F10-** Opens the File/toolbar bar
6. **F11-** Full Screen- Option

Try out these Time Saving Shortcuts Keys in Microsoft Word

Shortcut keys for A-J

1. (Ctrl-A) To Highlight everything all at once
2. (Ctrl-B) To "**Bold**" a word or letter
3. (Ctrl-C) Copy- Make a copy of text
4. (Ctrl-E) Center a Text
5. (Ctrl-F) Find a word/text
6. (Ctrl-H) Replace a word with another
7. (Ctrl-I) To "*Italicize*" a word or letter
8. (Ctrl-J) Justify move text freely
9. (Ctrl-L) Align text Left

Shortcut keys for L-Z

10. (Ctrl-P) Print
11. (Ctrl-R) Align text Right
12. (Ctrl-S) To Save a Document/File
13. (Ctrl-U) To Underline a letter or word
14. (Ctrl-V) Paste
15. (Ctrl-W) To Exit page
16. (Ctrl-X) Cut – Remove text completely
17. (Ctrl-Y) Repeat the same word
18. (Ctrl-Z) Undo Mistakes

Double Screen Effect

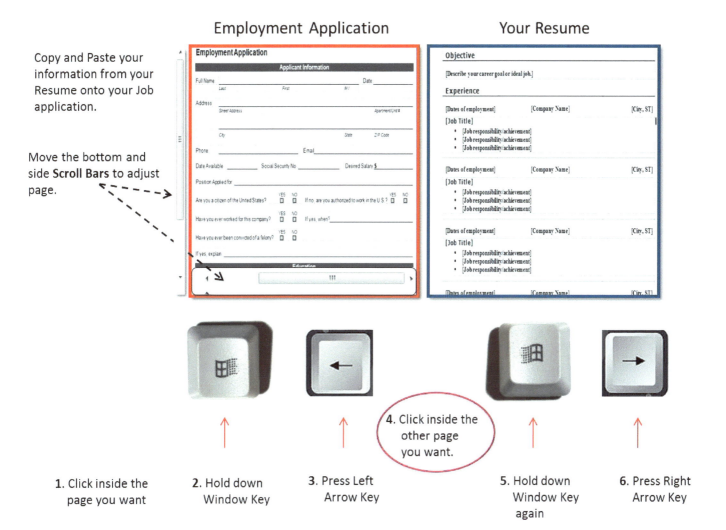

Employment Application

Your Resume

Copy and Paste your information from your Resume onto your Job application.

Move the bottom and side **Scroll Bars** to adjust page.

4. Click inside the other page you want.

1. Click inside the page you want

2. Hold down Window Key

3. Press Left Arrow Key

5. Hold down Window Key again

6. Press Right Arrow Key

Create Your "Resume" on Microsoft Word in 3 easy Steps

A. Click on "File"

F. Click on "Download"

1.

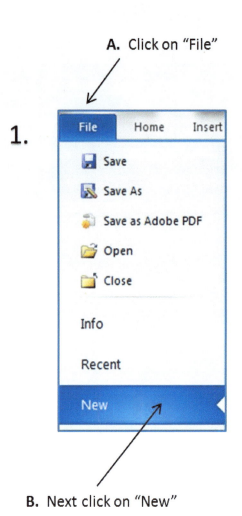

3.

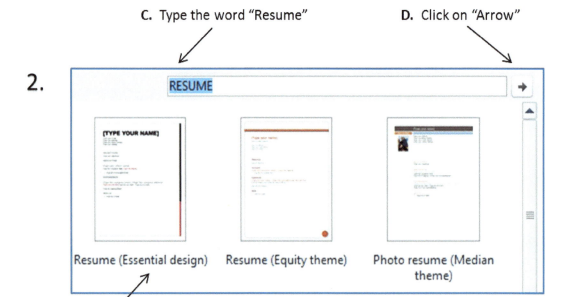

B. Next click on "New"

C. Type the word "Resume"

D. Click on "Arrow"

2.

E. Choose a resume style

(Open) Word documents in 4 easy Steps

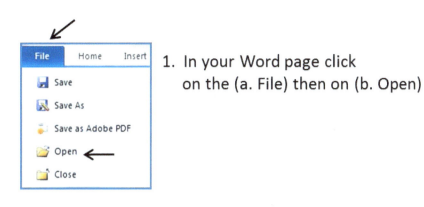

1. In your Word page click
   on the (a. File) then on (b. Open)

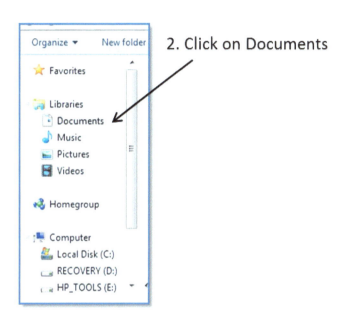

2. Click on Documents

(Open) Purpose

The purpose of "Open" is to re-open files that have been save Previously.

3. Type in Your File Name

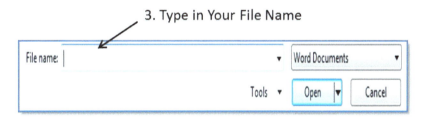

4. Click Open

(Save) Word documents in 4 easy Steps

1. In your Word page click
   on (a. File) then on (b. Save)

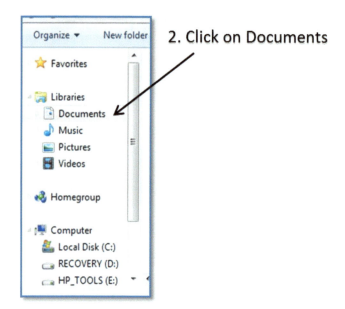

2. Click on Documents

(Save) Purpose

The purpose of "Save" is to save "New" documents for the first time.

3. Type in Your File Name

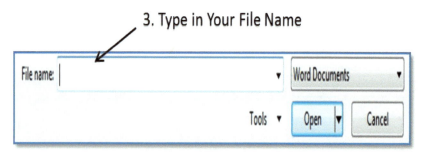

4. Click Save

(Save As) Word documents in 4 easy Steps

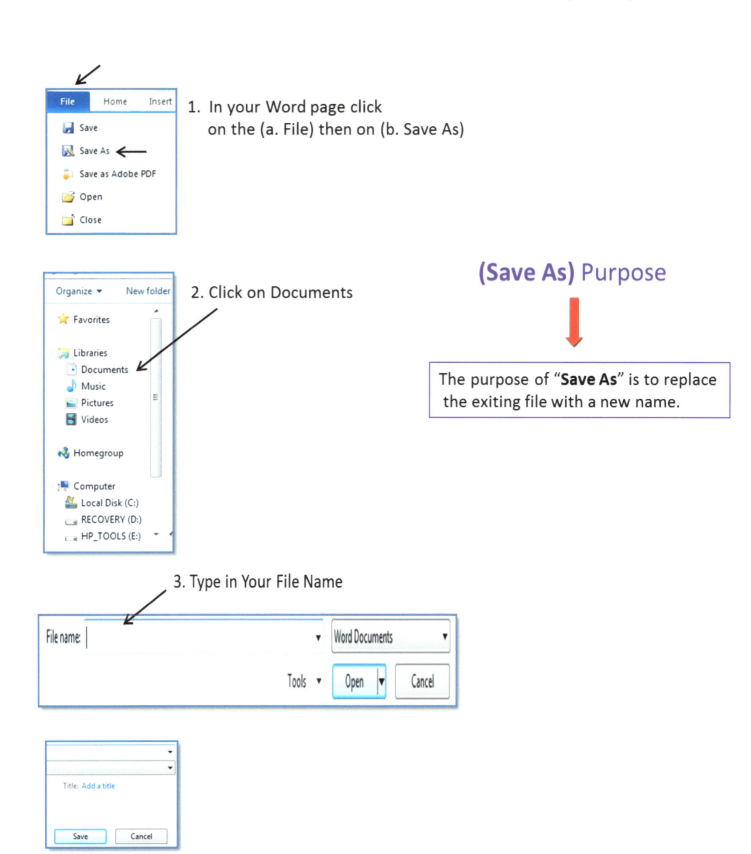

1. In your Word page click on the (a. File) then on (b. Save As)

2. Click on Documents

(Save As) Purpose

The purpose of "**Save As**" is to replace the exiting file with a new name.

3. Type in Your File Name

4. Click Save

(Print) Word documents in 5 easy Steps

1. In your Word page click on the File tab

2. Click on Print

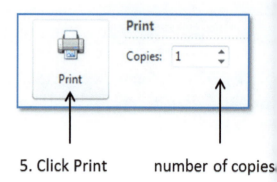

5. Click Print   number of copies

(Print) Purpose

The purpose of "**Print**" is to print out any page onto paper.

3. Click on (Print All Pages)

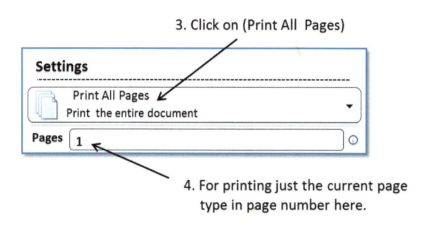

4. For printing just the current page type in page number here.

(Open) an Gmail account in 6 easy Steps

1. Go to Google website now click on Gmail.

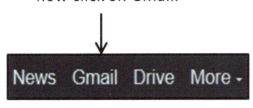

2. Click on Create An Account

3. Fill in your personal Information here.

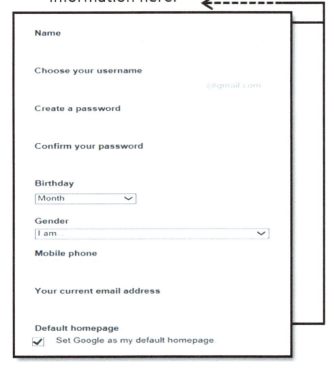

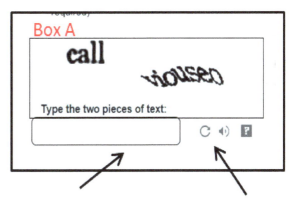

Box A

4a. Type exactly what you see in (Box A). Space between each word.

4b. If you do not understand Word(s) click "The Challenge arrow" for a new word.

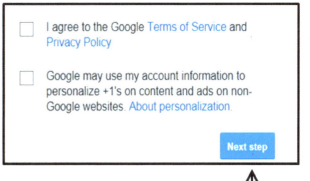

5. Read Google Term and services policy. Then Click "Next Step."

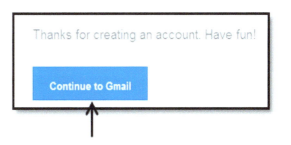

6. Click Continue to Gmail

(Open) a Yahoo account in 5 easy Steps

1. Go to Yahoo website now click on Mail.

2. Click on Create New Account

3. Fill in your personal Information here.

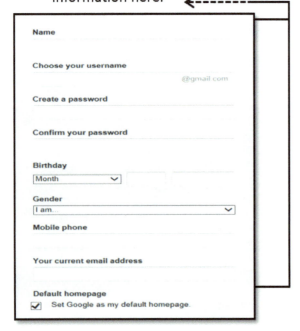

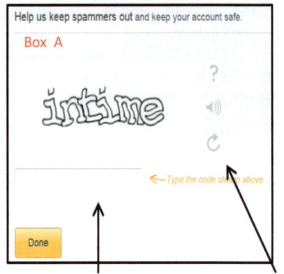

Box A

4b. Type exactly what you see in the (Box A).

4b. If you do not understand word(s) click the "the challenge arrow" for a new word.

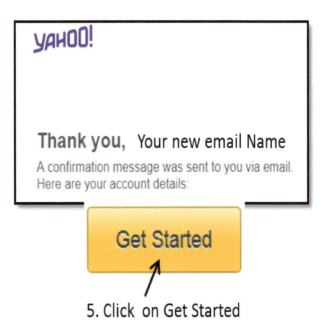

5. Click on Get Started

Saving Microsoft Word files on Yahoo Mail in 7 easy steps

1. Login into Yahoo; then Click on the "Compose" Button.

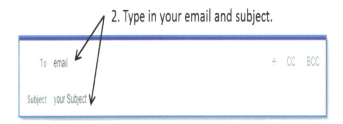

2. Type in your email and subject.

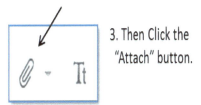

3. Then Click the "Attach" button.

4. Click on Documents

4. Double Click on your file

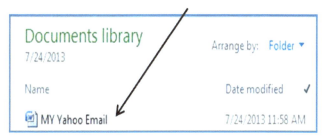

5. When file is "Attach" this symbol will appear.

6. Click Send, now Check your inbox for proof.

7. Click "Forward" Button to send to Others.

Saving your Word documents on Gmail in 6 easy Steps

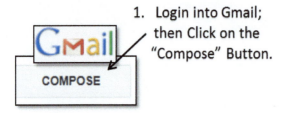

1. Login into Gmail; then Click on the "Compose" Button.

2. Type in your email and subject.

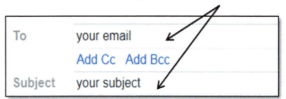

3. Then Click the "Attach" button.

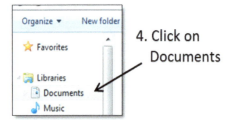

4. Click on Documents

4. Double Click on your file

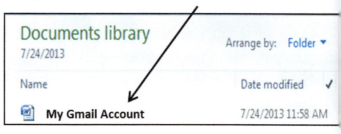

5. When file is "Attach" this symbol will appear.

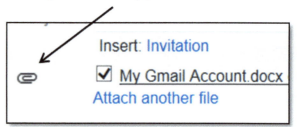

6. Click Send, now Check your inbox for proof.

Transferring Word documents into (Adobe) files in 4 easy steps

1. Click on File

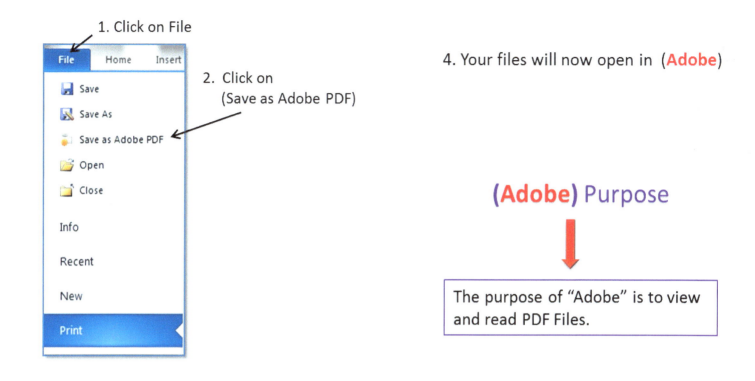

2. Click on (Save as Adobe PDF)

4. Your files will now open in (Adobe)

(Adobe) Purpose

The purpose of "Adobe" is to view and read PDF Files.

3. Type in your new file name

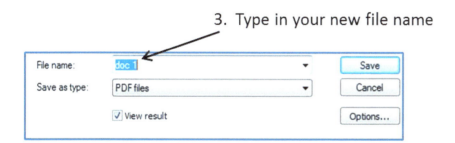

Open (Adobe) documents in 4 easy Steps

1. Click on File

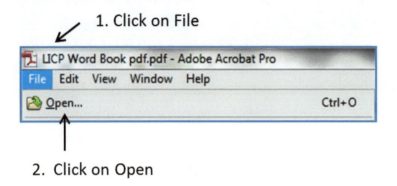

2. Click on Open

3. Type in your new file name

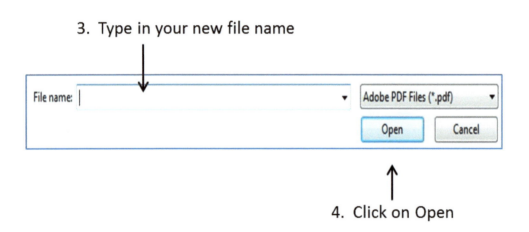

4. Click on Open

Save (Adobe) documents in 4 easy Steps

1. Click on File

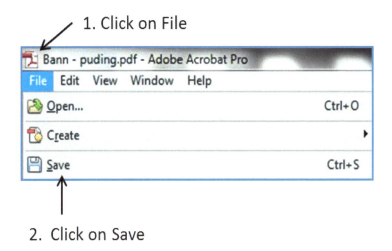

2. Click on Save

3. Type in your new file name   4. Click on Save

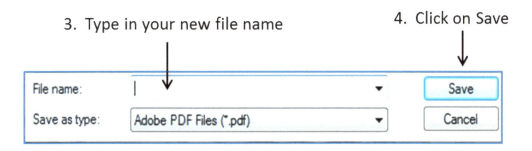

Print (Adobe) documents in 5 easy Steps

1. Click on File

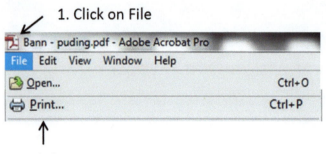

2. Click on Print

3. Type in Number of Copies

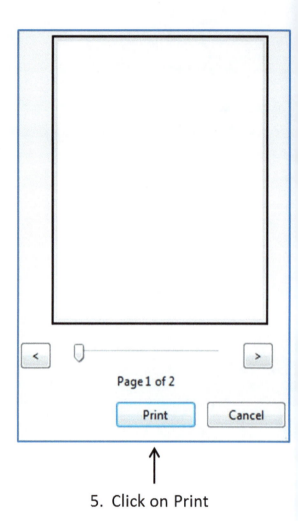

Page 1 of 2

5. Click on Print

4.

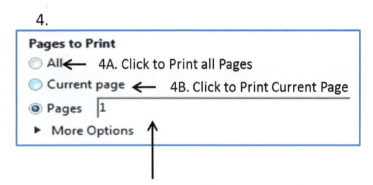

4A. Click to Print all Pages

4B. Click to Print Current Page

4C. Type in exact page(s) or range of copies
Example (1-3)

Print Website Page(s) in 6 easy Steps

1. Click on Tools Symbol
   * Top Right Corner

4.

4A. Click here to Print all Pages

4B. Click here to Print Current Page

4C. Type in exact page(s) or range of copies here. Example (1-3)

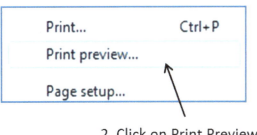

2. Click on Print Preview

5. Type in number of copies here

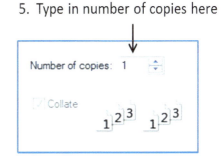

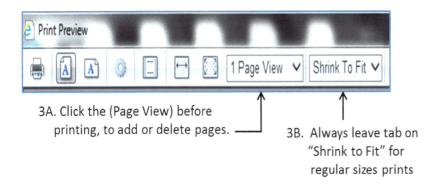

3A. Click the (Page View) before printing, to add or delete pages.

3B. Always leave tab on "Shrink to Fit" for regular sizes prints

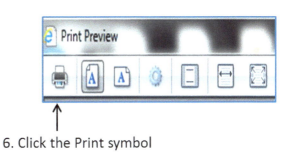

6. Click the Print symbol

Fast Printing tips to remember

When Printing email attachments always choose "download" for full size prints.

Download

When Printing PDF attachments always Click on "Display" for full size print outs.

See attachment

pdf_rept115207813767.pdf

Display

When you click on "**Display**" this symbol will appear at bottom of page , then click on the **print symbol.**

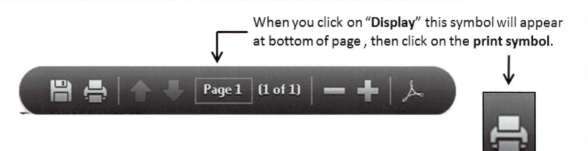

Print Symbol

Enlarger and Shrink Website Page in 3 easy Steps

1. Click on Tools Symbol
   * Top Right Corner

For Faster "Zoom" Power
Try (Ctrl +) for Lager
       (Ctrl -) for Smaller

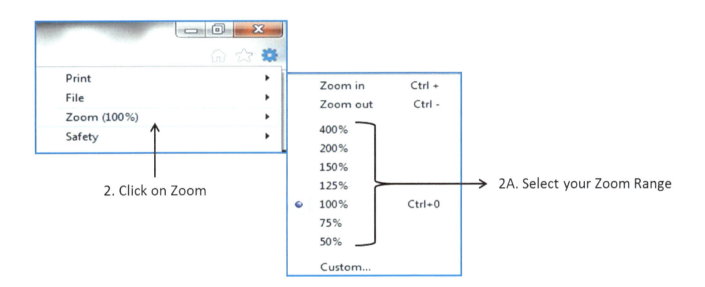

Print ▶	
File ▶	
Zoom (100%) ▶	
Safety ▶	

Zoom in	Ctrl +
Zoom out	Ctrl -
400%	
200%	
150%	
125%	
● 100%	Ctrl+0
75%	
50%	
Custom...	

2. Click on Zoom

2A. Select your Zoom Range

Translate Website Page into your Language in 3 easy Steps

1. Right Click
   anywhere on the
   web page you want
   to translate.

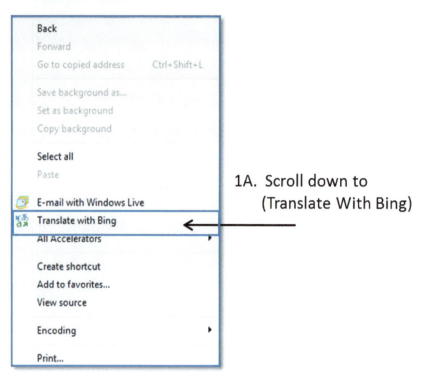

1A. Scroll down to
   (Translate With Bing)

3. Click on
   "**Translate this Page**"

2. Click here to choose
   your "**Language**" (A-K)

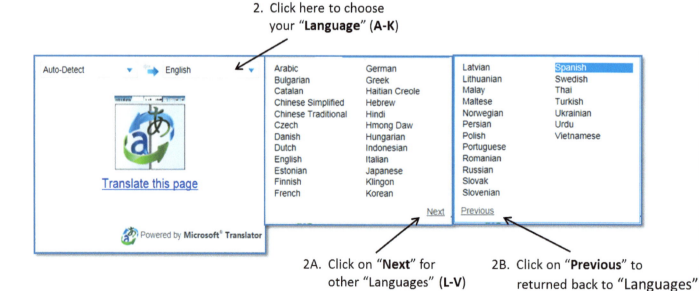

2A. Click on "**Next**" for
   other "Languages" (**L-V**)

2B. Click on "**Previous**" to
   returned back to "Languages"
   (**A-K**)

LICP

Library Instructional Computer Process

Library *(Volunteer)*

Power   Energy   Success

Questions or comments: Email: icp@computer4u.com